I0801035

IMAGES
of America

Logging Oregon's Coastal Forests

Ancient forests with massive trees once dominated Oregon's coastal landscape. Most of those trees survived the homesteading years of the late 19th century. The booming economy of the early 20th century, however, meant millions of those trees became logs. Fires in the 1930s burned millions more into snags valuable only as salvage. The war years of the 1940s suspended most logging, but in the 1950s, the industry returned with record outputs. By 1960, most of the ancient forest remained only as memory. (Courtesy of Clatsop.)

ON THE COVER: The elaborately posed image captures every aspect of logging for local markets in the 1890s. Oxen pull logs over a skid road. Loggers standing on springboards hold axes. Buckers in the foreground use crosscut saws. Some women and children take part in the event, but there's not a machine or hard hat in sight. (Courtesy of Tillamook.)

IMAGES
of America

LOGGING OREGON'S COASTAL FORESTS

Mark Beach

ARCADIA
PUBLISHING

ISBN 978-1-4671-6047-6

Published by Arcadia Publishing
Charleston, South Carolina

Printed in the United States of America

Library of Congress Control Number: 2023908181

For all general information, please contact Arcadia Publishing:
Telephone 843-853-2070
Fax 843-853-0044
E-mail sales@arcadiapublishing.com

Visit us on the Internet at www.arcadiapublishing.com

Contents

ACKNOWLEDGMENTS

The sources of photographs on the following pages include 10 personal collections and 15 agencies and archives. Captions give the names of the individuals. The agencies and archives are abbreviated as follows:

Bandon	Bandon Historical Museum
Clatsop	Clatsop County History Museum
Columbia	Columbia River Maritime Museum
Coos	Coos Bay Historical and Maritime Museum
Coquille	Coquille Valley Museum
Cowlitz	Cowlitz County Historical Society
Douglas	Douglas County Museum
ODOT	Oregon Department of Transportation
ODPR	Oregon Department of Parks and Recreation
OHS	Oregon Historical Society
OSA	Oregon State Archives
OSU	Oregon State University
Seaside	Seaside Historical Museum
Tillamook	Tillamook County Pioneer Museum
UofO	University of Oregon

I appreciate the prompt and professional help from staff at all the institutions above but want to say particular thanks to Ruby Fry-Matson in Tillamook, Rachel Lilley in Corvallis, Jim Proehl in Bandon, Liisa Penner in Astoria, Steven Beda in Eugene, and Laura Wilt in Salem.

Lloyd Lindley II sharpened my thinking about logging history. Janet Carter and Liz Cole brought their keen eyes to proofreading, asking questions about content along the way. Marie Scovell and her father, Cliff, one of the most vital of the old-time loggers, never failed with quick, clear answers to my questions. Thank you one and all.

Introduction

Remembering years of living in logging camps, Bob McIntyre described the camps as dreary villages of crowded mess halls surrounded by dirty shops and smelly bunkhouses. McIntyre recalled the skeletons of broken trees left to scar the landscape. "But," he said, "the moon brought out beauty in the hills. In the moonlight it seemed God pitied the weary land robbed by the hand of man."

McIntyre's words reflected a range of emotions regarding the logging industry on the Oregon coast. Even Ellis Lucia writing about his world of nude mountains and polluted streams remembered days in school when "the scream of the head rig and the glow of the wigwam burner were healthy signs of industry. Everyone lived with big timber, for the big woods furnished the sustenance of life itself."

Loggers of 100 years ago left their vivid memories in oral histories, diaries, and stories passed along to authors and families. Quotations from these sources appear in captions throughout the following pages, but images made by photographers roaming the woods made the book possible.

The first 30 years of the 20th century found professional photographers from cities visiting remote forests and logging camps. Some came assigned by newspapers and magazines. Others arrived under contract from the mill owning the operation and employing the men. Most, however, came as businessmen looking for customers. After a few days in the field lugging 50 pounds of equipment, they headed home to develop and print the new images. A week or two later, they appeared in camp on payday, looking for men who would buy prints before leaving for a night on the nearest town.

The early photographers were all craftsmen with technical skills and expensive cameras, but many were artists as well. They made the men in their images reveal the thrill, stress, and sweat of logging. They showed the bond between men and animals and the grit of men running huge machines. And they often turned their cameras to the larger scenes revealing logging as an industry: mills belching smoke, schooners loaded with lumber, and hillsides scarred with clearcuts.

The images made by those itinerant photographers have haunted me since I first saw examples almost 60 years ago.

Thank you for picking up this copy of *Logging Oregon's Coastal Forests*. I hope you enjoy reading it as much as I did writing it.

—Mark Beach
Manzanita, Oregon

Roving photographers focused on the enormous trees and the fearless men who cut them down. Images helped viewers understand what many loggers already knew: that the coast would someday run out of ancient trees. Falling the 600-year-old spruce in this image was just a morning's work for the two loggers. Today, one can see trees this old in a few parks and remote patches of protected wilderness. The rest remain only as weathered stumps scattered within young forests. (Courtesy of Tillamook.)

One

Astounding Trees

In 1915, more than 15 million people visited the world's fair in San Francisco, where the State of Oregon advertised the prosperity of its logging industry with the massive building shown above. Forty-eight Douglas fir logs, each 42 feet tall and 6 feet in diameter, supported the structure. The logs were cut, shipped, and installed with bark intact to ensure they all matched. (Courtesy of OHS.)

Oregon novelist Don Berry imagined how the coastal forest felt to early settlers when he wrote, "All around us an infinity of trunks stretched into the sky. The vastness, complexity, and density of the forest was like contemplating the number of stars. Endless ranks of the trees, silent and eternal, faced us. To learn humility, a man must stand in the midst of the Oregon forest." (Courtesy of the Rinehart family.)

Homesteader Charles Rorvik wrote, "Douglas firs covered the hills with a green mantle. Many stretched 300 feet into the air, clear of branches for the first 150 feet. The trees, straight as temple columns, often measured ten feet in diameter. Gloom hid the lower branches, but high above they lifted pyramid crests bright in the sunshine." (Courtesy of OSU.)

During their winter near Astoria, Lewis and Clark reported men returning from hunting who had measured a tree at the height of a man's breast 42 feet in the girth and at least 200 feet without a limb. They estimated the height of the tree at 300 feet. The tree shown here has a girth (circumference) of approximately 35 feet. (Courtesy of Norm Laknes.)

The coastal forest includes Sitka spruce, which lumbermen said had more varied uses than any other western wood. Sounding boards for pianos, tops for stringed instruments, and pipes for organs could all come from spruce. So could parts of ironing boards and refrigerators. Farmers used spruce for windmill slats and in poultry brooders. Spruce went into boxes and trunks, sash for doors and windows, and caskets. (Courtesy of OSU.)

STANDING TIMBER IN OREGON, 496,048,000,000 FEET.

Cut into lumber, this timber would fill 413,373 trains of 60 cars each or 24,802,400 carloads.

It would take 400 years for 40 sawmills, each sawing 100,000 feet of lumber a day, to cut this timber. Reforestation and natural growth would replace the timber so rapidly that, at the end of the 400 years, on the same acreage, there would be as much standing timber as there is today.

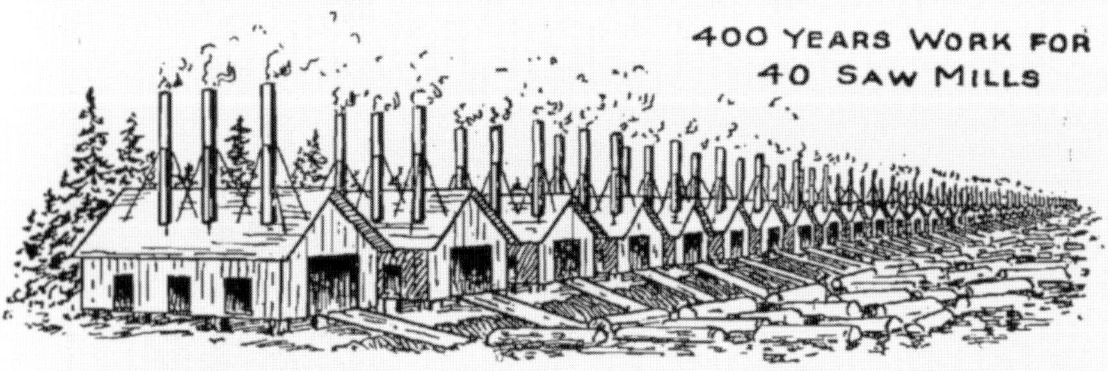

In 1912, the Oregon Immigration Commission published a booklet called *A Land of Opportunity* for home seekers, settlers, and investors. This image from that booklet captures the enthusiasm and optimism for what most Oregonians saw as endless forests. For 20 years, timber barons from cutover forests in the Midwest had assembled huge tracts of timber in Oregon and Washington. Excursion trains from Chicago and Minneapolis brought homesteaders, speculators, and experienced loggers to see for themselves. The booklet quoted a logger from Wisconsin who said, "The old growth Douglas fir averages 90 feet surface clear and running heavy to No. 1 logs. No woodsman could ever forget the sight." (Courtesy of OSU.)

Early in the 20th century, critics, including a few loggers, warned the timber industry was cutting trees four times faster than growing them. National progressive politics and regional economic worries urged more conservation and less harvesting. Meanwhile logging companies tried to sell cutover land to farmers. No one had learned the clearcut hillsides could grow nothing but trees. (Courtesy of Paul Clock.)

The lyrical words of John Muir and his friendship with Pres. Theodore Roosevelt helped build national support for conservation. Muir wrote about Douglas firs, "On a glowing horizon their majestic crowns tower over the forest. The oldest on a commanding ridge seem the very gods of the woods. In the evening light, their colossal heads made the stars sparkle on their branches like flowers." (Courtesy of OSU.)

For 14 months near the end of World War I, thousands of soldiers and thousands more civilians worked at breakneck speed to produce enough spruce lumber to make frames for airplanes. Military officers directed the work. The effort included buying timber lands, falling and bucking trees, and building roads and railroads to move the logs to mills. Specifications for lumber were so precise that the military built its own mill in Vancouver and started building two more mills, one in Washington and one in Oregon. When the war abruptly ended, army property became army surplus. Ads, such as the one above, reflected millions of dollars worth of infrastructure, buildings, machines, tools, and even land suddenly flooding the civilian market. Lumber companies scooped up everything from small tools to entire railroads at bargain prices. All that just as the military released soldiers and civilians onto the private market—ideal conditions to begin the logging boom of the 1920s. (Courtesy of the *Timberman*.)

The 1930s proved as dismal for the logging industry as the 1920s were rewarding. First, the economic depression squeezed the vitality out of the lumber market, then fires robbed the woods of trees. In just three years, the Oregon timber industry lost a third of its workforce. Everywhere, people saw empty camps, idle mills, and rusting equipment. Pulp sales fell by a third and lumber sales by two-thirds. Then the massive Tillamook Burn slammed the door already closing. Millions of old-growth Douglas fir trees, growing over thousands of acres, burned into huge clouds of smoke. Ships at sea and hikers on Mount Hood reported the clouds rising almost eight miles over the coast range. Fall rains finally doused the fire that had burned for almost two months. Learn more about the Tillamook Burn on page 39 and at the Tillamook Forest Center on Highway 6 east of the city of Tillamook. (Courtesy of Tillamook State Forest.)

The 15 years following World War II (1946–1960) proved a golden age for forestry. Mills during the war had worked below capacity because of a lack of logs and workers, and most lumber had gone for military needs. After six years of scarcity, and with the return of veterans needing jobs and housing, civilian demands boomed. Every market needed new homes, hotels, schools, hospitals, and libraries. Europe also needed wood to rebuild. Logging and lumber nationwide entered one more set of boom years. This image reflects the excitement of the times showing a 40-foot Douglas fir log en route to Oregon's Centennial Exposition in 1959. The prophetic words of the *Oregonian* newspaper back in 1901 still rang true: "Posterity may not bless the present generation for turning forests into fields, but while the change is being made the lumber business will place into circulation an immense amount of money." (Courtesy of Douglas.)

Two

CHOKER SETTERS AND WHISTLE PUNKS

Loggers use many terms unique to their profession. They "fall" trees, not cut them down. A tree on the ground has been "felled." Loggers buck felled trees into logs, set chokers on the logs, then yard the logs to a landing. They move from one show to another, the locations where they operate. This chapter introduces the words loggers used—and still use—to describe themselves and their activities, tools, equipment, and sites of operations. (Courtesy of Clatsop.)

While "logger" refers to the wide range of workers in the profession, each task, such as rigging, falling, and bucking, had its own name. Everyone within the profession used terms such as "high climber," "whistle punk," and "bull of the woods." And everyone knew about the large number of jobs supporting the men who felled trees. From the men who bought the forest to those who sold logs and lumber, complex logistics required dozens of skills and years of experience. Pay scales in the woods reflected job titles: cooks, teamsters, river drivers, and sawyers got the most. This image shows everyone from cooks to road builders to managers gathered in the hills east of Tillamook. Most of the men in the image—perhaps 90 percent—never used an ax except to cut personal firewood. All of them were loggers in the general sense of the term: men vital to the logging industry. (Courtesy of Tillamook.)

Cruisers use a tape measure to show the width of this huge spruce. After the tree has been felled and bucked, workers at the landing or mill will scale the resulting logs. Board foot measure serves as the basic unit for determining the value of logs. "Scaling" means measuring diameter and length, then determining board feet. Scalers compute the value of logs per thousand board feet, usually abbreviated as "MBF." (Courtesy of Tillamook.)

Decisions about the value of trees in part of a forest rely largely on the work of cruisers, professionals who estimate the quality and quantity of trees. Based on recommendations by cruisers, loggers selectively felled the most valuable trees in this stand and left others for later harvest. (Courtesy of Tillamook.)

This view looking south over Arch Cape in 1972 contrasts a mature forest with tracts that loggers have clearcut. The cape itself is part of Oswald West State Park, so it remains covered with trees hundreds of years old. Highway 101 passes through a tunnel under the cape. Logging roads among the hills to the east reach tracts where all trees have been cut, some several times. Clearcutting is controversial. Advocates argue clearcutting protects the safety of loggers, yields the most profitable timber, and prepares the soil for the next crop of trees. Opponents argue clearcutting robs the soil of nutrients, increases erosion and causes siltation in rivers and estuaries, destroys habitat for animals, birds, and fish, and looks ugly. (Courtesy of ODPR.)

The logging boom of the 1950s brought thousands of miles of new logging roads into Oregon's coastal mountains. The vertical aerial image above shows the roads more clearly than the oblique aerial on the opposite page. The pattern of roads shows a few mainlines leading to the nearest paved road and lots of spurs off the mainlines. Rails never entered this rugged terrain. Logs went out by truck. Highway 101 runs through Arch Cape near the right edge of the image as it does in the oblique image. The lightest parts of the image reveal the most recent clearcuts, the darkest part the most mature trees. Gray areas represent trees growing from seedlings planted following clearcutting. Trees in the gray areas range from five to 50 years old. (Courtesy of North Coast Land Conservancy.)

Near the top of the image, a high rigger leans from a spar tree above the cables used to stabilize the tree. Power from the steam donkey below pulls cables to yard hundreds of logs from where they were felled, limbed, and bucked to the landing, where loggers can load them for shipment to the mill. High-lead (pronounced "high-leed") logging from spars meant loggers could bring logs up from steep hillsides more easily than by dragging them over the ground. In this image, loggers stand on the donkey's sled facing away from the spar. The high-rigger chose a tall, healthy tree as a spar, climbed to limb off branches, cut off the top, then rigged it with cables. The high climber was one of the top men because he had to rig the spar securely so it would hold together so that nothing would slip. He also changed the guy lines and swung the blocks to line up with the new areas to log. (Courtesy of Tillamook.)

A spar tree was dangerous to climb and even more dangerous if it fell. Rigging consisted of blocks of huge pulleys of various sizes from a high-lead block to steel plates around the tree to reinforce the top. If it was a landing tree, the boom could come down in a tangled mess. The danger and confusion reminded loggers of the mast of a ship coming down in two or three pieces on a deck loaded with sailors. To avoid the need to climb and the risk of a falling tree, manufacturers developed the steel spar. A rail car carrying the spar on tracks in this image also carried a diesel donkey to power the rigging. In addition to the advantages of safety and speed, loggers could move steel spars to the next show on railroad tracks. See page 53 for more about steel spars. (Courtesy of Clatsop.)

Fallers undercutting this old cedar stand on springboards inserted into notches cut with axes. A springboard is portable scaffolding made using a tapered plank, typically a piece of two-by-eight-foot fir about six feet long, with a U-shaped steel plate bolted to one end. The plate has a sharp edge facing upward. The weight of a logger standing on the board forces the edge up into the tree to make the board a stable working platform. Springboards allow making undercuts above the butts of trees where the valuable logs begin. While hiking Oregon's forests today, one may see old stumps with springboard notches. Loggers in this image hold double-bitted axes with two sharp edges. Each edge was filed to a different angle, one for cutting cross-grain and the other for cutting with the grain. (Courtesy of Tillamook.)

Falling a tree starts with using axes and saws to undercut a wedge about a third of the way into the trunk. Sawing a back cut from the opposite side causes the tree to fall in the direction of the undercut. The huge fir in the image will fall close to where the photographer is standing. Two men using a long saw often called it a "misery whip." (Courtesy of Tillamook.)

Buckers prepare to buck the tree—to cut the tree into the lengths convenient to send to the mill. Bucking starts after slashing off limbs and the small top of the tree. Bucking crews use tools including axes, wedges, saws, and an undercutter, the device lying across the log. When suspended from the log, a grooved wheel at the lower end of the undercutter braces the saw cutting from below. (Courtesy of Clatsop.)

Choker setters have wrapped a thick cable around the log making it ready to haul to the landing. The cable is a choker, and the workers are choker setters. They refer to hauling as yarding. Whether logs are dragged over the ground by oxen or a steam engine or swung from a high cable, they are yarded to the landing. (Courtesy of Clatsop.)

Choker setters have choked the logs and have started to snipe the log in this image. The snipe is a bevel on the leading edge of the log to help prevent it from getting stuck on rocks, roots, and small stumps while skidding over the ground or a skid road. Ground lead logging required snipes. Loggers also sniped the leading edges of donkey sleds for the same reason. (Courtesy of Tillamook.)

Turning a felled tree into logs starts with creating slash by cutting limbs off the felled tree. Slash may also include small trees with no market value and the top (smallest) part of felled trees. Sometimes loggers make piles of slash to clear the ground for replanting and then burn the piles. Other conditions call for leaving slash spread around the ground to save money and feed nutrients as it decomposes. (Courtesy of the author.)

Loggers have bucked this log from a massive spruce ready to set chokers and yard it to the landing. The fourth logger from the left holds a peavey, a sturdy pole with a spike and hinged hook at the end used to turn and control logs. Loggers controlling logs floating in rivers and mill ponds use the longer pike poles shown at the top of page 32. (Courtesy of Clatsop.)

Choker setters and snipers break for a photograph after preparing this log for yarding. The men wear caulk shoes (sometimes spelled calk but always pronounced "cork") and tin pants they have stagged, best seen on the man at the end of the log holding the axe. Thick canvas pants waterproofed with paraffin felt like wearing pants made of tin. Stagging—cutting a few inches off the legs—helped prevent catching in branches, or slash. For the same reason, loggers wore suspenders, not belts. Caulk shoes have short metal spikes like hobnails in the soles to keep from slipping on trees and logs. Loggers must have sure feet to work in the woods. When they jump, maybe carrying 50 pounds of rigging, they do not want to hit a slick spot on a log. High-top shoes protect from rocks and maybe cuts from their own ax. Loggers protected their caulks by not stepping on anything metal. Also, they called them shoes, not boots. They claimed fishermen, cowboys, and farmers wear boots, but loggers wear shoes. (Courtesy of Clatsop.)

The young man in this image holds a line over his shoulder used to blow a whistle on a steam donkey. On command from the donkey driver, tugs on the line blew the whistle to send messages to loggers over a wide area. Two short blasts meant "come back on the haul back line." Three short blasts meant "come easy on the main line." The dreaded five long blasts brought news of an accident. Loggers called operators of the signal "whistle punks." Old-time loggers said they could hear whistles from dozens of engines all over the woods and claimed they could recognize the sound of the whistle from their specific show. Near one of the giant steam donkeys with thundering voices, they would have to shout above the roaring inferno inside the firebox and the groans from the huge drums as they hauled or slacked tons of cables thick as arms. Today's loggers use 20 signals adopted by the Pacific Logging Congress—the same signals used 100 years ago. (Courtesy of Clatsop.)

Oxen are seen here yarding a turn of logs along a skid road, also called "corduroy road." Small logs laid across the road make the turn easier to pull by keeping logs off the ground. Skid roads work best on routes no longer than two miles and for turns with logs shorter than 30 feet. Men driving the oxen often relied on boys not old enough to punk whistle to grease the skids ahead of the oxen. Managing oxen on skid roads required a team of three loggers. The driver, called the "bull puncher," kept the animals pulling hard and together. Teams had a hook tender, who chained up the load, and a hand skidder, who kept the load secure during yarding. See also page 43. (Courtesy of Tillamook.)

Loggers have mounted a steam donkey on a sled. A donkey is an engine using rotating drums to pull cables for yarding logs, loading logs, rigging trees, and moving equipment. With rigging attached to a distant tree, a donkey on a sled could pull itself toward its next task by reeling in a line. Developed in the 1890s using steam engines, later models used gasoline or diesel engines. The donkey in the image below has a roof protecting the operator from falling limbs and small logs. Cordwood at the lower left feeds the fire to keep up pressure in the boiler. An engine running all day could burn a cord of wood. Legend says loggers called the machines "donkeys" because they did not deserve ratings by horsepower. (Above, courtesy of Paul Clock; below, courtesy of Tillamook.)

Teams of horses have yarded Douglas fir logs to a landing next to the backwater of a river flowing toward the mill. A landing is a site holding multiple logs ready to transport to a mill. The ground crew will roll the logs down the ramp into the water. The driver standing on a floating log will use his pike pole to guide the log into the flow of the river. (Courtesy of Clatsop.)

Loggers call logs placed in an orderly pile a "cold deck." Cables from the donkey in the background hang from a spar tree to lower logs onto the cold deck ready to load onto railcars or trucks. The cold deck in this image appears stacked on a railcar no longer on rails, so it was used only to hold the bottom logs off the ground. (Courtesy of the Rinehart family.)

Logs seeming to float in the air or actually floating in water need restraints called "booms" to keep them in position. Cables attached to the bottom of the boom help lower the log into place. Cables attached to the sides and top help steady the boom itself. (Courtesy of Clatsop.)

Logs chained end-to-end in water form booms to enclose logs in rivers and mill ponds. The booms in this pond for a mill in Garibaldi hold millions of board feet of logs sorted by species and size. A railroad brought most of the logs in this image from logging shows along the upper Nehalem River. (Courtesy of Tillamook.)

Moving logs on trains across streams and over canyons required trestles strong enough to carry cars loaded with tons of logs. Most structures needed to last only until operations stopped all along the line, so they were built quickly using nearby materials. Building a cribbing trestle, as below, simply involved stacking logs at right angles until reaching the required height. Building a pile trestle, as above, required pounding logs into the soil until they reached solid footings. Cribbing trestles went up faster and needed fewer machines to build. Pile trestles required longer logs, more machine time, and better engineering, but could reach greater heights. Remnants of old trestles are common sights along the grades of abandoned logging railroads. See more about trestles on page 65. (Both, courtesy of Tillamook.)

Drivers standing on floating logs use pike poles to keep logs aligned as they drift toward the mill pond. The crew of drivers following logs along the bank or walking on the logs are driving the logs, therefore the term "log drive" for the operation. Log driving required the most skill and meant the most danger of all logging jobs. One old-timer said river loggers considered themselves the aristocracy of the industry. They called woods loggers "timber beasts with meaningless jobs" compared to the perseverance and endurance needed to overcome the river. Many snags in the background of this image suggest this drive was part of a salvage operation after a fire. Railroads and trucks moved logs to mills faster with less cost and danger than driving them in rivers, making log drives obsolete during the 1930s. (Courtesy of Tillamook.)

The mill pond at a Trask River mill holds fir logs driven from upriver logging shows. Mill ponds could range in size from relatively small, shown above holding just a few hundred logs, to many acres holding thousands. The flow of the Trask River, not a railroad, brought logs to this pond. Lumber at the other end of this early mill must leave by ship or wagon road. (Courtesy of Tillamook.)

Loggers sometimes built dams across streams and small rivers to hold logs in the ponds behind the dams. Opening the dams created a flood to carry the logs downstream. The term "splash dam" described the sudden rush of water. At one time, almost 200 streams in the Oregon coastal mountains had a splash dam. Learn more about splash dams on pages 70–73. (Courtesy of Coos 992.8.0375.)

Steep grades and sharp curves in the coast range sometimes prevented moving logs by rail. With enough water at the top of the hill for a sudden flush, logs could surf the wave down a flume. Daring loggers would sometimes hop a log for the thrill of the ride. The flume above had grades from 10 to 15 percent and curves of 17 and 20 degrees. (Courtesy of Tillamook.)

If old-time loggers looked at this image, they might say the log could scale 8,000 or 10,000 feet. Just one tree that size might yield 50,000. An acre of old-growth might yield half a million. When a logger said feet, he referred to board foot, a unit of measure one foot square by one inch thick used by the forestry and wood products industries throughout America. The measurement is usually abbreviated as "BF." (Courtesy of Tillamook.)

Nature has several ways to turn healthy trees into snags—standing remnants of previous good health. Wind is the most common. High wind can snap trees, leaving a snag such as in the image at left. As wind breaks the tree, the top can snap smaller trees as it falls. The top of even an average fir or spruce can weigh several tons. As the wind crests a ridge line, it can accelerate to mow down multiple trees on the downslope. Fire can kill thousands of trees, leaving the skeletons in the image below. Wood in fire-killed trees can stay firm for several years, depending on tree species, weather conditions, and insect invasion. After a fire, logging companies and forestry officials launch salvage operations quickly to save what lumber they can. (Left, courtesy of the author; below, courtesy of Tillamook.)

In 1933, a fire destroyed almost 12 billion board feet of prime timber on the north Oregon coast. Economists at the time claimed the fire was the worst economic disaster in American history. Thousands of personal stories made the event vivid. Lucy Dougherty wrote in her diary that "it rained charred leaves and needles. Embers lay all over the ground and roofs. Ocean waves left rows of deposits on the beach. As late as Labor Day people bathing in the surf came out blackened instead of cleansed." Called "the Tillamook Burn," the fire began in August on the east side of the mountains and burned 240,000 acres until rain put out the last of it two months later. For the next 20 years, loggers salvaged over 400,000 snags. Most revealed marketable timber covered by the burned bark. Trucks carried logs over 55 miles of new forest roads to county roads and then to mills throughout Northwest Oregon. From the early 1950s until the 1970s, thousands of Oregonians planted 72 million seedlings in the scarred landscape. Their legacy is today's Tillamook State Forest. (Courtesy of the US Forest Service.)

Stumps remaining after loggers fall trees, and logs on the ground, become havens for seedlings and underbrush. The general term "nurse log" covers all situations where rotting wood supports new growth. Hemlocks seem especially fond of growing from nurse logs. And nurse logs remind everyone that trees nourish the forest even after they die. Nurse logs are potting soil helping the forest to sustain itself. (Courtesy of the author.)

Loggers had reputations for trying everything, including foul language, to get the logs moving. The words helped pop off emotion. It would not help to say "tutti-frutti" or "Jiminy Christmas." Sometimes it helped to take off a hat and stomp on it while cussing. Then when the log would finally get moving, everything would feel happy again. Loggers only stayed mad so long as the situation required. (Courtesy of Tillamook.)

"Gyppo logger" is a slang term for loggers who are independent contractors rather than employees of a mill or owners of timberland. Author James LeMonds quotes the wife of one gyppo outfit describing the enterprise: "Start off with an impulsive, stubborn, hard-working guy with logging in his veins, add a couple of pieces of haywire equipment bought on credit, and you've got your gyppo. He's underfinanced most of the time and continually plagued by closing operations in hot weather or by deep snow, or by machinery breakdowns, or by shortage of trains to carry logs to market. A surplus of creditors means he runs his outfit all day, welds his machinery back together between supper and darkness, then builds a road when the moon comes up. As for his wife—well, it's no life for a softie, but you can bet there's never a dull moment." Ken Kesey's classic novel *Sometimes a Great Notion* is about a family of gyppo loggers on the Oregon coast. (Courtesy of OSU.)

The language of logging sometimes failed to express how some people felt. Mary Manary watched as her husband and sons logged and "the magnificent living trees cracked to earth, their feathery greenery dragged through dust and mud. Men bucked the great hulks into lengths and, now quite dead, loaded them into cars and dumped them in the mill pond. It was depressing to think of all the small animals and birds, scattered and scared, forced to find their ways to new homes to escape the menace of man." (Courtesy of Tillamook.)

Three

Ox Teams and Steam Donkeys

Handling oxen along a skid road could be treacherous. The grease monkey had to know when to speed up the load by lubricating the skids and when to slow it down by covering the skids with dirt. If a load moved too slowly, it could come to a sudden stop. If a load moved too quickly, it might overtake the bull puncher and team. Logging lore includes numerous stories of men and animals injured or killed by a runaway load. (Courtesy of Columbia.)

From the 1880s through the 1930s, loggers relied on crosscut saws. Saws ranged from six to 12 feet, generally twice the diameter of the tree being felled, as shown in this image. Saws required two men and were made and sharpened according to whether falling hard or soft wood, green or snag. The introduction of crosscut saws in the 1880s cut falling time in half while also improving safety. (Courtesy of Columbia.)

Experienced loggers say crosscuts properly sharpened produce shavings, not dust, and sing as they cut. The song is a smooth swish, swish, swish. The crosscut meant loggers could fall two trees a day in big timber. Wedges pounded into the tree as the saw cuts deeper prevent the tree from buckling and trapping the blade and help guide the direction of the fall. (Courtesy of OSU.)

The equipment required to fall this spruce includes springboards, saws, axes, and wedges. Bottles hanging from springboards contain kerosene for the saw. Kerosene dissolves the sticky pitch and tar that makes the saw bind as it passes through the tree. One can near the ground has kerosene to refill the bottles. A jug of drinking water stands nearby. In hot weather, every man drank at least a gallon of water per day. (Courtesy of Clatsop.)

Loggers agree that there is a lot of procedure to falling a tree. They must know which way it leans, then find the best lay for it, all the while keeping safe. They must hit the spot where they want it to fall, not just dump the tree anyplace convenient but where it might break. The money comes from a tree properly felled. (Courtesy of Tillamook.)

Loggers felled trees with singing saws long after they had replaced animals with steam and steam with gasoline and diesel. But by the 1950s, the internal combustion engine had become small enough to carry into the woods. Equally important, engineers had developed chains with teeth similar to saws and bars to guide the chains through sprockets in the engine. During the 1950s, the chainsaw transformed logging as profoundly as had the steam donkey 60 years earlier. Chainsaws reduced the size of crews while increasing the production of logs. Within just a few years, one man with a chainsaw could fall more than three men using axes and hand saws. This image shows loggers demonstrating a two-man Disston saw in about 1950. The Disston company had made top-quality crosscut saws for almost 100 years. When one logger saw this image, he said his father had one of those saws for a while. He said it weighed 100 pounds and took two guys to operate once they got it started, which might take half the day. (Courtesy of the Forest History Society.)

Tree trunks on the ground could lie higher than the loggers bucking them. Depending on their length, logs from a tree this size could yield 2,000 board feet of lumber. Bucking saws such as in this image were shorter than crosscuts and designed for one man. (Courtesy of Clatsop.)

Huge steam engines made many logging tasks easier, but men still had to operate saws by hand. Soon, some handy mechanic figured out how to use steam to operate oscillating blades for bucking. By the 1920s, two-cycle gasoline engines ran drag saws, such as the one seen here, for bucking. The logger bending over is guiding the blade as it finishes the cut to prevent the teeth from hitting the ground. (Courtesy of Seaside.)

Job titles in the woods clearly specified function, rate of pay, and place in the hierarchy of workers. Titles included woods boss, faller, choker setter, bull buck, and peeler. Bull whackers drove the oxen, while grease monkeys helped control the surfaces of the skids. Each yoke of oxen could pull about 4,000 pounds. The elaborately posed image here captures every aspect of logging in the 1890s. (Courtesy of Tillamook.)

Two new techniques have entered the woods in this image from near Coquille: oxen have yarded logs to a landing, but horses take over from there to take the logs out; rails have replaced skids. The wagonload of logs rolls on flanged wheels hugging the rails. The wooden rails will not last any longer than skids but will serve well enough until loggers move to their next show. (Courtesy of Coquille.)

When ground conditions allowed using wagons instead of skid roads, loggers preferred horses to oxen. Horses replaced oxen as they are faster, easier to handle, and lack horns. Teamsters handling either horses or oxen had skills equal to cooks and sawyers and so received equal pay. (Courtesy of Tillamook.)

Don Pizer remembered when two logs slipped from their chokers and started down the hill, coming at him end over end like a pair of toothpicks: "I dove behind a stump as they bounded down the ridge. One flashed a shadow across me as it passed. The other crashed against a stump so hard I thought it would rip it from the ground. My legs shook for the rest of the day." (Courtesy of Clatsop.)

When the pressure to meet production goals got too strong, sometimes the donkey crew would plug holes in the boiler, screw the top-off valves down, stand in the bight of the line, and holler to the whistle punk to start the rigging. The boiler might explode like an old steamboat. Along with plenty of skill in the woods, there was no shortage of stupidity. (Courtesy of OHS.)

Crews for steam donkeys included two or three men to haul water and split cordwood. Crews tended to have teenagers learning the trade and older men lacking energy for other tasks. Regardless of age, they considered themselves holding inferior jobs. The teenagers especially claimed splitting for firewood "ain't logging." (Courtesy of Tillamook.)

It always seemed a contest between the irresistible force, the men trying to move the log, and the immovable object—the log which did not want to move. A man either made the log move or was moved himself down the road. The bosses told the men if they cannot move the log, they will get men who can—that is the way it works. (Courtesy of Clatsop.)

Loggers in this image have used two donkey engines to yard logs to the landing next to railroad tracks. Logs are placed uphill from the tracks, ready to roll onto railcars headed for the mill. Several men have stagged their pants, while others simply turned them up to avoid the mud and tangles. (Courtesy of Clatsop.)

Powerful steam donkeys allowed high-lead logging using a cable, called a "skyline," rigged from the spar pole at the landing to a stump or tree near the falling area. Loggers made spar poles by limbing and topping a tree they thought was strong and in the right place. When high-lead replaced ground yarding early in the 20th century, it almost doubled production. And before high-lead logging, dragging logs to hilltop landings caused enormous environmental damage. One logger remembered how logs skidding up to the spar tree gouged huge ruts. Rainy weather filled the ruts with liquid mud. Choker setters often waded waist-deep in mud by quitting time. Every turn of logs pulled down the canyon also moved a muddy mixture of rocks and debris. As the logs burrowed into former creek beds, they formed moving dams of brown water. Another old logger remembered brooks once splashing clean and clear from the canyons. With hills stripped of trees and underbrush, sludge and rocks tumbled down the channels formed by logs dragged to the landing. He said he learned firsthand about soil erosion. (Courtesy of Tillamook.)

This ad from 1913 reflects the constant impact of technology on the logging industry in the Northwest. Beginning with the first mills in the 1850s, making lumber for buyers beyond their local market, technical developments have reduced the number of employees needed to fall the same number of trees and mill the same number of logs. From the logging standpoint, first came the crosscut saw to help the ax, then steam to replace animal power, and then gasoline to replace much of human power. Each development reflected the promise of the ad for "Small Crew, Large Capacity." From the sawmill standpoint, steam replaced wind power and waterpower, band saws replaced circular saws, and electricity replaced steam. Every change on both sides of the log also came from the development of new materials, such as stronger steels and tougher rubbers, as well as from inventive ideas and rewarding business practices. (Courtesy of Tillamook.)

In the image above, a camp perched on a hilltop east of Tillamook requires powerful locomotives to reach the summit to take out logs produced by nearby crews. Locomotives had boilers and pistons designed to place maximum weight onto driving wheels but still needed occasional help on steep slopes. In the image below, loggers have run a cable from the locomotive to a steam donkey for a helpful tow up the 45-degree grade. One logger called steam donkeys and locomotives "monsters built to devour the wilderness." (Both, courtesy of Tillamook).

Clearcuts remain controversial, especially when they blemish views such as this over the fairway of a golf course. But since 1972, Oregon has required landowners to plant seedlings on forestland after harvest. Restocking must begin within 12 months and be complete by the end of the second growing season. The number of seedlings required depends on the land's productivity. The most productive land requires 200 trees per acre, moderately productive 125 per acre, and 100 trees per acre in the least productive areas. By the end of the fifth growing season, seedlings must be healthy and free to grow, out-competing surrounding vegetation. This image was taken when the clearcut was in three stages of regrowth. The left third has seedlings two years old. The middle third has just been cut, so it has not yet been replanted. The right third shows trees about five years old. Restocked trees appear a lighter gray than old growth and cover the land at uniform heights. Both advocates and critics sometimes call restocked lands tree farms instead of forests. (Courtesy of Linda Cook.)

Logging crews tended to attract experienced loggers from the same nations or states. Countries included Sweden, Finland, Denmark, and Norway. States included Michigan, Wisconsin, and Minnesota. This image shows men from North Carolina using their state nickname for Tarheel Logging in Coos County in about 1914. (Courtesy of Douglas.)

Loggers have sniped the Douglas fir logs for yarding over the ground instead of in the air with high leads. Loose cables once connected to the chokers yarded the logs to the site. A nearby steam donkey has provided power to roll the logs onto the railcar. Cordwood in the foreground will fuel the donkey and possibly the train engine as well. (Courtesy of the Rinehart family.)

The danger of every phase of logging and millwork has always been well known. As loggers use their tools and equipment, they stay on constant alert for danger. The risks grow when working on rough terrain, in bad weather, and in sites remote from medical care—all common conditions. Death was usually brutal but quick. A man might die under a rolling log, in a tangle of flying rigging and chokers, from the kickback of a tree as it toppled from its stump, or from falling limbs crashing to the ground. Loggers were also exposed to possible train wrecks, collapsing trestles, and exploding steam engines. Today, the Occupational Safety and Health Administration (OSHA) says "the hazards in logging present a significant risk to employees in operations throughout the country, regardless of the type of timber logged, where it is logged or the end use of the wood." In this image, loggers pose in 1901 outside a small mill near Nehalem. (Courtesy of Tillamook.)

Loggers liked to brag about their agility, strength, and taste for danger. Here, they show off up five boards—about 20 feet up the snag. Keeping his place as strongest among the strong, the boss in the suit jacket poses on the highest springboard. Loggers recalled the old days when the boss of the woods would not burden himself with an army of foresters, surveyors, tree markers, and other fern hoppers, all rushing uphill and down carrying barometers, binoculars, microscopes, relief maps, bug killers, and test tubes. Some also say the new emphasis on growing logs as farm crops destroyed the glory, glamour, and excitement of a career in the woods. (Courtesy of Tillamook.)

Four

Rails, Rivers, and Roads

The early days of logging in the coastal forests found most mills close to their supply of trees. Animal power could bring logs to mills, which cut lumber for homes, barns, schools, churches, and other local needs of the homesteading years. A few large mills, located along major waterways and called "cargo mills," cut lumber for shipping to San Francisco and foreign ports. (Courtesy of Tillamook.)

Using animals to haul logs short distances often involved building skid roads from logging sites directly to mills. Many mills preferred horses to oxen for this task because horses could also more easily pull wagons, as seen near the center of this image, to deliver lumber. (Courtesy of Coquille.)

A few loggers and timberland owners, moving in the 1890s to the Northwest, brought memories of steam tractors used to plow midwestern prairies. When they saw steam donkeys yarding logs, they realized how much more versatile they could be on flat ground mounted over wheels instead of sleds. The tractor in this image is little more than a small steam donkey on wheels. (Courtesy of Tillamook.)

Loggers used rails even before steam engines entered the woods. Two horses could not pull a monster such as the one above along a skid road but could move it easily over rails. Using horses meant workers could set rails at any convenient width without relying on standards for equipment built elsewhere. (Courtesy of Tillamook.)

When distances from logging sites to rivers grew too long to haul logs by oxen or horses, forest owners built railroads to the next show. The short lines carried logs to mainline rails connecting directly to mills and could return with people and supplies to camps and landings. (Courtesy of Tillamook.)

Until steam came to the woods, horses and mules hauled Fresno scrapers to grade for roads and railroads. Operators could set blades to scrape at different levels depending on the condition of the soil. Graded soil went into the buckets behind the blades and then was dumped nearby when the buckets were full. (Courtesy of Tillamook.)

Steam increased the power of machines to build grades and trestles for trains. As railroads took over from animals, logs moved from stump to mill faster, more dependably, and at less cost than using animals or rivers. Steam also took over the job of running mill machinery from water. Steam mills could have more power, handle larger logs, and be portable if necessary. (Courtesy of Dolly Jasper.)

In the early 20th century, newspapers throughout western Oregon clamored for railroads to haul logs and lumber. An editorial in the *Yaquina Bay News* claimed, "Build the railroads and the vast country will become the greatest wealth-producing region on the face of the earth." (Courtesy of Tillamook.)

Loggers took pride in their ability to balance on logs. Bragging rights came from riding logs while standing, whether loaded on railcars, floating in rivers or mill ponds, or rushing down a flume. Many described the security of feeling caulks bite into the bark to ensure their feet had a strong grip. Cooks did not wear caulks, but the apron on the man in this image showed cooks' place in the hierarchy. (Courtesy of Tillamook.)

Each locomotive had an engineer, a fireman, and two brakemen. The men knew a log-hauling locomotive was smoky, dangerous, and often bought used well beyond its expiration date. Somehow luck and skill kept them in service as they proved no place too remote and no forest safe as they chased the timber. (Courtesy of Tillamook.)

In this image, a trainload of logs from the Nehalem River drainage waits on a siding near the mill in Wheeler. A steam donkey provides power to lift each log and then slide it down the ramp into the mill pond. The main line of the track remains open for trains hauling logs south to mills in Brighton, Garibaldi, Hobsonville, and Tillamook. (Courtesy of Port of Nehalem.)

Multiple creek beds and steep hillsides in the rugged coast mountains made building grades for railroads expensive and time-consuming. Trestles built with logs from nearby trees crossed the distances faster at a lower cost. Trestles could go up fast partly when crib logs (above) and pile logs (below) rested directly on the ground instead of on footings. But contact with the ground invited rot, making many trestles unsafe after just a few years of operations. Cedar would resist rot longer than fir but was too valuable to hold off the market except for special situations. Douglas fir was abundant, but strong markets sometimes meant resorting to hemlock, with little value and more prone to rot. One study showed trestles of cedar lasted 15–20 years, Douglas fir 8–10 years, and hemlock 3–6 years. (Above, courtesy of OSU; below, courtesy of Tillamook.)

Engineers used steam donkeys to power piledrivers while building trestles over creeks and marshes. Cables from the donkey drum raised the huge pistons and then dropped them onto logs placed vertically in the ground below the water line. The logs used for pilings came directly from nearby forests without treatment with preservatives. Port Orford cedar, shown below, stood up even longer than western red cedar, so it was used for thousands of pilings in southern Oregon until the Japanese market for the Port Orford variety developed in the 1920s. Cants for decking and ties, made from fir or spruce, often were treated with a preservative before leaving the mill. (Both, courtesy of OSU.)

No one knows how many trestles loggers built in the coastal mountains, but estimates range in the low thousands. Many with hasty construction, poor engineering, or rotted materials—or some combination of the three—led to frequent accidents. Rumor said train crews would walk across a trestle they thought might fail, letting only the engineer risk staying on board. The accident in these two photographs happened in 1912 east of Bandon when the train started to cross a new trestle for the first time. Six men died when the train fell 100 feet into the creek bed below. Accidents did not always involve deaths but did always involve the cost of salvaging the train and the loss of several weeks of production. (Both, courtesy of Bandon.)

In the 1910s, high-lead logging almost doubled output because logs moved through the air instead of dragging over the ground. Bosses paid bonuses for volume. Paying for volume encouraged recklessness because every second counted in the age of efficiency. Moreover, many operators ran with poor equipment, including weak and damaged rigging, which increased the danger. Rusty cables might snap without warning, hurtling around like Paul Bunyan's whip. (Courtesy of William Gibbons.)

Four steam donkeys mounted on sleds and loaded onto railcars indicate a large operation somewhere in the woods. Cables used as draw lines, attached to drums on the donkeys and run through the points of the A-frame cranes, will lift logs from the landing to place them on railcars or trucks to move to the mill. (Courtesy of Clatsop.)

Railroads were the primary way to move logs from landings to mills from the 1890s through the 1930s. One estimate claimed that from 1910 through 1929, rails increased timber cuts in the West by 200 percent. But loggers needed a huge number of trees to support the costs of building and operating a railroad, so they felled trees faster than ever and deeper into the forests. (Courtesy of Tillamook.)

Fewer markets combined with more powerful truck engines and the low cost of building roads instead of railroads ended the era of railroads during the 1930s. During World War II, millions of tons of railroad engines, cars, and the rails themselves were hauled from logging operations and melted down to become steel for ships, tanks, and cannons. (Courtesy of Tillamook.)

From the earliest days of logging in the colonies, loggers relied on water to move logs to mills. This image shows Oregon loggers continuing the tradition. The steam donkey has brought logs to the bank of the river, where the donkey engineer will push them into the water. (Courtesy of OSU.)

Once in the river, a boom or dam contains the logs until the water rises high and fast enough to carry them downstream to the mill. Floating logs often meant photo opportunities for loggers and their ladies. In addition to standing calmly on a floating log, all six people in this image had to walk from the bank over several other logs to get into position for the camera. (Courtesy of OSU.)

Storing logs at the riverside meant falling and bucking could continue throughout the year, even when low rainfall meant low water in the rivers. Scenes such as this might contain millions of board feet. Despite loggers' best efforts to align logs parallel to the bank, tangled inventory, called a logjam, often became four or five logs deep. Dynamiting a jam was the most dangerous of all logging operations. (Courtesy of OSU.)

Loggers built splash dams on dozens of coastal streams from the 1880s through the 1940s. River drivers considered themselves elite because they felt exposed to more danger, exhibited more bravado, and got more pay than even high climbers cutting spar trees. Drivers liked to brag that they were as agile as squirrels and could ride bubbles all the way to the mill. (Courtesy of Columbia.)

Depending on the height of the dam and the topography upstream, a reservoir behind a splash dam might hold thousands of logs. One driver remembered standing on logs floating in fast water. He said many drivers drowned and many more had legs or bodies broken. If a man got injured, other drivers would help however they could and then leave him on shore. A driver who died was simply forgotten or maybe had his shoes hung on the nearest tree. Regardless of the danger, the logs had to move. Another driver claimed old-time river rats forget the cold days of backbreaking labor and remember only the excitement of tumbling logs rushing toward the sea. He said their caulks are dull, their clothes dry, and their tools dusty in museums. (Courtesy of OSU.)

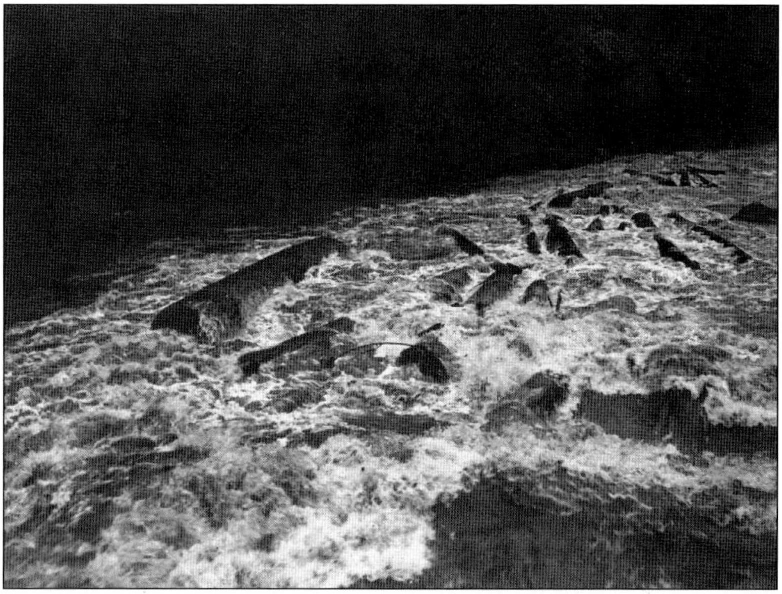

Logs released by splash dams caused enormous environmental damage as they rushed and tumbled downstream. The freshets carrying logs washed out spawning gravels, flushed away sandbars and docks, and brought tons of silt into estuaries. Organizations of fishermen and farmers protested to state authorities loudly and often. (Courtesy of OSU.)

The use of splash dams decreased during the 1930s as roads and log trucks moved farther into the woods but increased during World War II, when loggers could not get fuel and supplies for trucks. The Oregon Legislature finally outlawed splash dams in 1956. The damage caused by some of the dams remains to this day. (Courtesy of OSU.)

As logs drifted into the relatively quiet waters of estuaries, booms strung between pilings helped guide them toward a mill. Mill ponds in estuaries, perhaps holding a million board feet, were little more than larger versions of the enclosure in this image. Pilings dating from logging days still dot Oregon's coastal rivers and bays. (Courtesy of Tillamook.)

Drivers for Wheeler Lumber Company have started to build a raft of logs in Nehalem Bay. Cables laced among the logs form a floating platform ready to support more logs placed on top. Rafts were designed for tugboats to tow into the ocean but proved hard to hold together, especially when crossing the bars, even after the construction of jetties in the 1910s. (Courtesy of Tillamook.)

Gasoline engines driving trucks and hauling trailers with solid tires appeared in the woods at the same time as automobiles appeared on local roads. Power typically came from the same 20-horse engines found in Model T Fords. Trestles with planks for trucks cost less to build and maintain than those with rails for trains. Animal power could not have pulled this huge cedar from the woods. (Courtesy of Tillamook.)

For 18 years, Frank Hutchinson worked for the Oregon Department of Transportation making architectural drawings. His images captured the beauty of bridges, roads, and parks. This image, made in 1943, shows log trucks about to turn onto a road winding through untouched forest. Did the image make Oregonians miss bygone days or look forward to falling more trees? (Courtesy of ODOT.)

Collectors of antique trucks as in this image say loggers bought hundreds in the 1920s as military surplus. The trucks weighed two tons empty and used hard tires, requiring plank roads to stay out of the mud. Going faster than 20 miles per hour on those tires might void their warranty. (Courtesy of Tillamook.)

Loggers often wanted evidence of huge logs shipped from their show. This monster waits for delivery to the Whitney mill near Tillamook. Whitney Logging scaled this spruce, cut in 1918 for the Spruce Production Division (see chapter seven), at almost 13,000 board feet. (Courtesy of Tillamook.)

When two old-timers saw this image, one said the truck is a "hearse for trees," while the other said it is a "truckload of money." Their comments reflect opinions about logging Oregonians have held ever since logging began to checker the landscape and dominate the economy. The evolution of the Oregon Department of Forestry (ODF) reveals those opinions in the form of legislation and regulations. Established in 1911, ODF's mission focused on preventing and fighting forest fires. Political support for those tasks, both in Oregon and nationwide, sprang from fires in Idaho that burned three million acres in 1910. The Tillamook Burn of 1933 brought the importance of fire control to Oregon's front door. Since then, the mission of ODF has grown to include protecting watersheds, requiring replanting after logging, recreational uses of forests, and managing thousands of acres of state forests, primarily in Clatsop and Tillamook Counties on the north Oregon coast. (Courtesy of ODOT.)

As the logging industry boomed during the 1920s, highway officials noticed increasing road damage caused by heavy trucks and began setting weight limits. In 1941, ODOT created 50 weighing stations to check carriers of logs, poles, and pilings to control the costs of repairing damage caused by illegal loads. Heavy loads also meant longer loads, so trailers often did not stay within the lanes of tight curves. During the 1950s, highway officials reported that unprecedented demand and record high prices for logs and lumber caused an increase in overloaded trucks. Moreover, profits from overloads far exceeded the nominal fines imposed by local courts. The cost of accidents involving log trucks just added to the cost of maintaining roads stressed by heavy loads. Throughout the 1950s, half of all motor vehicle accidents in Oregon involved log trucks. (Courtesy of OSA.)

Five

Sawmills and Schooners

The jumble of logs and lumber in this image reflects the essence of sawmills for local markets along the coast in the 1880s and 1890s. Horses stand ready to deliver materials to construction sites. This chapter captures the spirit of these small mills while also describing the place of larger mills serving outside markets. The chapter begins, however, by showing the ways Native Americans used lumber made with hand tools. (Courtesy of Tillamook.)

Indigenous people stood on frameworks, similar in function to springboards, to start falling trees above the butt. Sharp sticks, stones, and antlers gradually whittled away the wood until the tree fell. Fallers preferred cedar because it rotted more slowly and split more easily than other species. (Courtesy of Paul Huckfeldt.)

Workers guided logs felled near rivers and bays toward shorelines for yarding, then to sites for making lumber. Local Native Americans did not have horses or other draft animals, so they yarded using their own muscles. But they did make skid roads, as shown here, and choker lines from woven cedar bark. (Courtesy of Paul Huckfeldt.)

Indigenous workers created canoes from cedar logs. After cutting the log in half, they split off a board to create a flat bottom. Using an adze, they carved out the center. Filling the cavity with water kept hot by heated rocks softened and stretched the wood before adding struts. Sometimes, bow and stern pieces were carved and added separately. (Courtesy of Paul Huckfeldt.)

Native Americans along the Oregon coast used stone hammers to drive wedges made from elk antlers to split boards from cedar logs. Each board represented many hours of work. Most of the boards went into houses and decks (seen on the following page). Thinner boards became shingles on roofs—the ancestors of today's cedar shingles for roofs and siding. (Courtesy of Paul Huckfeldt.)

Lodges built along rivers and bays relied on wood harvested from nearby forests or salvaged as driftwood on the beach. Lodges usually sheltered several families—often as many as 40 people. Some lodges had a floor below ground level, as in the image above. Others used the ground as the floor, as seen in the image below. Both types of structures required long, flat slabs for roofs and siding. The abundance of western red cedar in the coastal forest meant indigenous people could also build structures such as shacks for drying meats, sweat lodges, and decks. Cedar pilings resisted rot as well as providing sturdy support. (Above, courtesy of Clatsop; below, courtesy of Paul Huckfeldt.)

The image above shows a cabin built by homesteaders with the same materials as those used by indigenous people. Rough-cut cedar slabs form the roof and siding. The homesteaders, however, have the advantage of the saw leaning against the house. The tops of stumps reveal trees were sawn, not chopped. Battens (narrow strips of wood) covering seams between boards and materials for fencing seem milled instead of cut by hand. The image below shows more evidence of a local sawmill. The roof and siding appear the same as in the image above, but lumber for the windows, steps, and porch seems milled. The first mills were operated by water wheels. Logs came from nearby timber during dry weather, and mills started cutting when fall rains raised the streams. A typical mill produced about 2,000 feet a day. (Both, courtesy of Tillamook.)

Many early mills were small enough to set up near logging sites. Portable mills used two circular saws, shown in the center of this image. The diameter of each blade could measure as much as six feet, but blades so large were thick to cut evenly. A thick blade meant a wide kerf (the width of the cut made by the saw), causing wasted wood in the form of sawdust. (Courtesy of Douglas.)

Huge band saw blades cut larger logs than even the biggest circular blades. Band saw blades weigh less and are thinner than circular blades, so they require less power but require more maintenance. Operators can change band saw blades more easily than circular blades, adjusting the tooth pitch to the species and conditions of logs. And band saw blades have thinner kerfs than circular blades, so they create less waste. (Courtesy of Gary Katz.)

The Davidson family built this mill on the Siuslaw River as Oregon entered the booming lumber years of the 1950s. The mill included the wigwam burner near the right of the image, a standard feature of mills of the era. Wigwam burners were basically huge burn barrels whose fires burned continuously. Conveyor belts or pipes using compressed air fed bark, sawdust, planer shavings, and chips from shredded slabs into the top of the structure and into the fire below. Screens at the top let the smoke out but not the cinders and sparks. Anyone living within a mile of a burner in those days, especially if downwind, remembers the constant smell of wet wood burning. In the 1960s, resistance to the constant smoke brought pressure to close the burners. But burners were already becoming obsolete as mills learned to turn waste into profit. Paper mills and landscapers could buy chips, heating companies could make pellets for stoves, and mills themselves could make particle board. What little waste remained might burn as fuel to turn turbines generating electricity. (Courtesy of Siuslaw National Forest.)

Before rails crossed the coastal mountains, large markets lay by water down the coast to California and across the oceans in Asia, Europe, and South America. Lumbermen called the mills producing for outside markets "cargo mills." Because cargo mills brought in money, they encouraged settlement by offering jobs for cash. And because mill owners wanted control over the cost, design, and handling of ships, they started building their own. (Courtesy of Bandon.)

Mariners cruising the Northwest coast in the late 18th century realized the value in the huge trees they saw on shore. Douglas firs, some straight and free of limbs for 200 feet, made perfect masts. Smaller trees worked for spars, especially spruce because of its high tensile strength. Europeans arriving in the next century to farm the land saw trees as obstacles instead of resources. (Courtesy of Bandon.)

In the late 19th century, cargo mills near major ports such as Marshfield (today's Coos Bay), Bandon, Newport, and Astoria began building ships designed to carry lumber. The schooner *Randolph*, built near Bandon in 1910, was among the first to have a gasoline engine. In 1915, the *Randolph* was running in ballast (without cargo) at low tide when it capsized entering the Bandon bar after hitting the south jetty. (Courtesy of Bandon.)

The C.A. *Smith* was a steam schooner built for Simpson Lumber in the Kruse and Banks shipyards in North Bend. This image shows its launch in 1917. The vessel sank in 1923 after striking a rock going out from Coos Bay while carrying 1.5 million board feet of lumber. Kruse and Banks built 67 schooners, tugs, minesweepers, and even a steam paddle-wheel ferry during its 40 years in business. (Courtesy of UofO.)

The Hammond Lumber Company operated the mill in this image on the shore of the Columbia River near Astoria from 1908 until it burned in 1922. The mill in 1908 was about half the size as seen in this image. At the time of the fire, the mill occupied 21 acres, employed about 500 men, and produced 500,000 board feet per day. The railroad on the trestle bringing logs to the pond at left in the image was the mainline of the Astoria & Columbia River Railroad running 60 miles east. Spur lines ran south into the hills of Clatsop and Columbia Counties, opening vast tracts of timber for mills along the Oregon side of the river. Lumber could go by rail connecting to Portland and points east or by schooner to California and foreign markets. The railroad also brought logs to the schooners, as seen in the upper-left corner of the image, for shipment to Hammond mills in California. The Astoria mill never reopened after the fire. The prosperous years of the 1920s

increased the number and sizes of lumber shipments from coastal ports. Large steamers, many destined for foreign markets, carried loads far greater than the coastwise schooners of the 19th century. Mill owners pressured civic leaders and port authorities to secure funds to dredge harbors and build jetties. Officers and equipment from the Army Corps of Engineers became familiar local sights. A lumber industry publication urged local leaders to try for 16-foot channels by applying to congressmen to put an item into the Rivers and Harbors Bill, ensuring the item went before the board of engineers, ensuring orders for a survey and estimate, and then convincing Congress to appropriate the money. The channel of the Columbia River from its mouth to Portland is currently maintained at 43 feet. (Courtesy of Clatsop.)

Dimensional lumber is piled on a loading dock at Coquille. Until the early 20th century, most mills cut lumber to actual sizes. A two-by-four for local markets was actually two by four inches. During the 1920s, larger mills started cutting the nominal sizes found in today's lumber yards. Standard nominal sizes opened national markets and reduced weight, therefore also shipping costs. Today's nominal two-by-four actually measures one and a half by three and a half inches. (Courtesy of Coquille.)

Port Orford cedar is on a loading dock in Bandon. Loggers have split the logs lengthwise in a process called "riving." Rives weighed much less than whole logs, so they were easier to load, ship, and handle at mills. They also appealed to mills serving international markets needing lumber milled to metric standards. (Courtesy of Bandon.)

In 1913, the *Oregonian*'s description of logging on the Coquille River said six steamers and nine sail vessels carried lumber over the Coquille River bar. The article said 100 million feet would ship that year. This drawing shows 400,000 board feet of lumber forcing the schooner *Advance*, built near Bandon in 1902, low in the water as it heads for the bar. (Courtesy of Tillamook.)

The steam tug *Vosberg* was one of dozens operating on the Columbia River and many smaller rivers entering the ocean. Tugs had two primary functions: towing schooners over the bar or upriver to mills and towing barges and log rafts to California. Some tugs also carried supplies and passengers to isolated ports. The *Vosberg* worked from 1902 to 1912 from its base in Nehalem Bay. (Courtesy of Tillamook.)

Barges have a long history in the lumber industry because of their ability to carry huge loads at low cost. As tugs grew more powerful and the California market boomed, barges joined schooners in the coastwise lumber trade. Lumbermen also used barges to move equipment, supplies, and sometimes entire camps. The barge in this image carries 3.5 million board feet, beyond the capacity of even the largest schooner. (Courtesy of Bandon.)

The shallow drafts of barges, even when fully loaded, made them more suited than schooners for crossing bars into the ocean. But barges lacked their own power and steering capacity, making them harder to handle. The barge seen here is about to lose 25 percent of its load of four million board feet after hitting the south jetty of the Coquille River. (Courtesy of Bandon.)

Several companies in the 1890s tried rafting logs from ports on the coast to markets in California. Executives thought towing rafts would cost less than sailing schooners. But rafts often lost their loads when they broke up in the ocean because they were merely one layer of floating logs enclosed in booms and a few chains. A few years later, logger Simon Benson and an engineer he hired developed the technique shown in this image. The engineer showed Benson how to build a floating foundation, shaped like half of a huge football and then fill it with logs. Benson called the result a "cigar raft." One raft might be a thousand feet long and hold five or six million board feet. Tons of chain wrapped around the raft held the logs in place. When workers opened the foundation, the force of the lower layers of logs trying to float squeezed the entire pile into the chains, making the raft stable enough to tow over the bar and withstand ocean conditions. (Courtesy of Library of Congress.)

For a century starting in the 1850s, following the California gold rush, thousands of ships carried billions of feet of logs and lumber from the forests of the Northwest to San Francisco. Many of those ships were small schooners with shallow drafts, sometimes with retractable centerboards, built specifically to cross the shallow bars of rivers along the Oregon coast but too small to cross the open ocean. Many also carried passengers, making San Francisco a more important destination than Portland. This image captures the work of unloading at wharves lining the San Francisco Bay. Longshoremen in the image provide most of the power with a steam donkey in the background adding the rest. Many of the logs became pilings supporting the wharves. One visitor called San Francisco "Venice built on pine" because the whole central city swayed over pilings the size of masts pounded into the mud. Among the pilings, ships served as stores, restaurants, and residences. (Courtesy of Library of Congress.)

Six

PANCAKES, DONUTS, AND PIES

At the turn of the 20th century, most logging camps seemed like larger versions of the typical homestead: buildings made from shingles and slabs, horses and oxen in the yards, and families and single men gathered with hand-operated saws for turning logs into lumber. Small shows and mills had operated for almost 50 years, but their size was tiny compared to the operations coming during the next 30 years. (Courtesy of Coquille.)

By the 1920s, new corporations owned vast tracks of timber in the coastal mountains. Large logging camps dotted hillsides and riparian plains. The housing for over 100 workers shown above was perched over a mountain at Whitney's Blue Star camp east of Tillamook. The largest building contains a mess hall and kitchen. Other large buildings house equipment, maintenance, and administration. Rails connect the camp to the Whitney mill on Tillamook Bay. (Courtesy of Tillamook.)

Most logging camps contained buildings for only a few years until nearby timber ran out. No camps were more temporary than the tent camps built by the US Army in 1918 (see the following chapter for details). Smoke from the wood stoves and wash on the lines suggest that it is Sunday at this camp for the spruce soldiers near the Miami River east of Garibaldi. (Courtesy of Clatsop.)

A typical camp in the 1920s served about 150 men. The camp might have five sides, each needing one windfall bucker, twelve fallers and buckers, one head bucker, four choker setters, one hook tender, three chasers, three engineers, one fireman, one whistle punk, two loaders, one foreman, and one powder monkey for about 150 men in the woods. The rest of the employees worked in kitchens, maintenance, and administration. (Courtesy of Clatsop.)

The photographer of this image found in just one shot a way to capture the size of a donkey on a sled, the convenience of housing next to the tracks, and the clatter, creaking, and smoke of a logging camp. Machines used to lift logs could also lift an entire house and place it on a flatcar ready to move to the next camp. (Courtesy of Clatsop.)

Camp kitchens fed anywhere from 50 to 200 men breakfast and dinner and sent them into the woods with lunch. Each man needed 5,000 to 8,000 calories per 10-hour day. Calories came from cereals, bread, biscuits and donuts, bacon and other meats, and gravy and potatoes. Desserts meant canned fruits along with pies and cakes. Cooks tried to provide fresh milk but never failed to ensure all the coffee a man could drink. (Courtesy of Clatsop.)

Loggers said they could work in the mud and rain risking life and limb, do without showers, and sleep in a drafty bunkhouse, all with few grumbles. But if there was a cutback on the quality and quantity of meals, they would quit immediately and spread bad words about that camp's food. The camp with the best food got the best men. (Courtesy of Clatsop.)

Loggers spoke of cooks with awe and appreciation. Memories included mountains of food and the cook not allowing talking during meals. No talking meant fewer fights and getting out of the mess hall fast. Loggers were typically out the door 10 minutes after sitting down. (Courtesy of Tillamook.)

In oral histories, loggers often refer to each other by nicknames. Maybe a crew had "Four Finger" who got too close to a saw and "Froggy" with a big mouth. "Straight Rail Jim" stood with his hands behind his back. "Soup Bones," "Drop Pot," and "Wooden Shoe" worked in the kitchen. When asked for real names, many said they only knew the nickname. (Courtesy of Tillamook.)

By the 1920s, loggers started expecting camps with clean bedding and hot water for bathhouses. After working all day, they only wanted to eat and rest. Bosses put lights out at 9:00 p.m. and rang a wake-up bell an hour before dawn. When cooks asked what time to wake the men, the bosses said whenever they are asleep. (Courtesy of Tillamook.)

Loggers called some bunkhouses bull pens because they held 10 young men like bull pens in baseball. There was always a stove in the middle to keep the place hot so that wet clothes hung on the wall would dry overnight. It always seemed too hot or too cold. This image shows the inside of a tent typically sleeping eight men with an old Civil War stove in the middle. (Courtesy of Clatsop.)

Most men wore wool underwear and usually went to bed with it wet. They might not take it off for three months. Boot grease, kerosene, sweat, pipe smoke, and musty clothing combined for an oppressive aroma. On Sundays, some men heated water on the stove in old kerosene cans to give themselves and their clothes a quick wash. The rest lived with their stench. (Courtesy of Cowlitz.)

From the 1890s to the 1920s, the workday for loggers shrank from 12 to 10 to 8 hours. The 12-hour day meant Sunday was the only time off, but 10- and 8-hour days could mean an hour or two off in the evening—especially in the early evening of the Oregon winter. Shorter workdays also meant better-rested men, resulting in safer working conditions. (Courtesy of Cowlitz.)

Men who sharpened saws ranked with chefs in status and pay for employees in camp. Everyone knew the teeth must align properly or saws lead one way or another and cut wavy lumber. Points must be wider than the blade because the blade can crack if friction with the log makes it too hot. Loggers claimed an overheated saw could fly to pieces in a sudden rage. Crews called a man with a feeling for saws a "true filer." Without the feeling, they claimed, nothing can teach him to file. Sawyers in the image above work in a tent with a frame for a kerosene lamp hung from the ridge pole. The men below work in more permanent surroundings and perhaps only with good daylight, with no artificial light in sight. (Above, courtesy of Clatsop; below, courtesy of Cowlitz.)

Logging required hundreds of machines and tools kept in good working order. These images show mere glimpses into maintenance operations. Crews had axes and saws to keep sharp, cables and hooks to repair, and steam engines to clean, grease, and test. Maintenance included blacksmithing, as shown by the anvil above and the crew below. The massive engines on donkeys demanded constant attention because failure stopped production and, much worse, risked injury and death. The network of belts from machines toward the ceiling shows this machine shop ran on a central steam engine, though light fixtures suggest the boiler could generate electricity too. (Above, courtesy of Clatsop; below, courtesy of Cowlitz.)

A camp made up of train cars in the 1920s was an entire community for 100–150 men. Trains could include two mess halls, a kitchen, food storage, a commissary, a library and card room, bunk rooms, a boiler and turbines for electricity, toilets and showers, maintenance, and staff offices—all on separate cars 14 by 64 feet. Following the shelter cars came flatbeds loaded with donkeys and other pieces of huge equipment. (Courtesy of Clatsop.)

Starting in the 1920s, camps with housing for married men might have included a grade school looking like hundreds of others serving rural communities. Teachers said kids liked the style of a one-room school where they read while the teacher divided her time and where older kids taught younger ones. Teachers liked working at camps because loggers trained their children to obey, pay attention, and work hard. (Courtesy of Tillamook.)

Crummies were familiar sights on logging railroads. The crummy was any vehicle taking people to and from the woods—bosses, cooks, buckers, drivers, everyone all together, who would just hop on for the ride. Crummies helped end isolated camps by making it easier for employees to live in towns with high schools, churches, stores, telephones, and professional services, maybe even a movie theater. Convenient transportation also led to larger mills close to more workers. When power saws took over for axes and whips and crummies let men live in town, camp cookhouses no longer provided 5,000-calorie days. Some loggers complained gasoline engines made men soft and settled down. They missed the rough conditions of camp life free from the rules of polite society. (Both, courtesy of Clatsop.)

Logging camps located on the main line of a railroad in a river valley could consolidate logs from spur lines east in the hills and move the logs to mills west along the bays. This base camp on the Nehalem River served the short line shown in the middle of the image, four spur lines 30 miles inland near the crest of the Coast Range, and seven mills along Nehalem and Tillamook Bays. The camp in this image included bunkhouses and a mess hall for single men at the right and houses for married employees along the river. Large buildings on the left held storage areas and maintenance shops for logging and railroad equipment. Many base camps had a post office and school. The property today is the Nehalem River Ranch, producing pasture-raised meats and supporting new farmers. Headquarters camps served as staging areas for huge amounts of food,

coffee, fuel, and supplies, administrative offices, and jumping-off points for salesmen, doctors, dentists, and photographers. The head cooks controlled buying and shipping kitchen inventories to satellite camps upriver along with hiring and firing dozens of other cooks. Locations such as the one shown above had exclusive contracts with surrounding farmers and dairymen. Sometimes they owned their own herd of cattle to make sure they had the required daily pound of beef per man for several hundred men. Key employees included bakers because the men thrived on bread, pancakes, donuts, pies, and anything else high in calories and sugar. Bakers felt proud of their craft and might not have talked to the meat and potato cooks. (Courtesy of the Stevens family.)

Young, single men formed most of the population of the typical logging camp until the 1920s. Women were unusual and children more so. Occasionally, the kitchen and administrative staff might have families. In those rare cases, camps located completely on trains included a school car, as shown in this image. When it came time to move the camp, cranes would load bunkhouses on flatcars. Some were little three-room houses about 14 by 36 feet built to fit on the trains. Owners got to take only dishes from the cupboard. There was no electricity or plumbing so no wires or pipes. The wood stove went along but not the firewood. At the next camp, cables scooted the buildings off the flatcars onto the waiting platforms. (Courtesy of Seaside.)

In 1923, the Manary Logging Company built an entire logging camp on a barge along the Siletz River. The lower level included a kitchen, mess hall, commissary, and rooms for kitchen staff. The second floor had 10 bedrooms, each holding four men; sanitary rooms; and a filing room at the back with windows to allow maximum light. Running water came from a tank on the roof, and electric power came from a generator on deck. Company records called the barge Camp 11, but everyone from mill owners to whistle punks called it "the Ark." They called the watchman during the off season "Noah" regardless of his name. The image below shows the back of a camp on a train, again with a well-lit filing room at the rear. (Both, courtesy of OHS.)

During the first three decades of the 20th century, dozens of professional photographers made at least part of their livings making images at logging sites. Loggers, many from other countries, bought prints to send home showing life in America. Photographers often arrived on Saturday to sell prints from pictures taken during a previous visit. Saturday was payday, so salesmen wanted to deal with the men before they took their cash to town. On Sunday, cameras could capture scenes, including visiting wives and children, and photographers made sure to show plenty of people (customers) in the images. Archives throughout the Northwest include thousands of prints and scans of images made by those tenacious photographers. (Courtesy of Tillamook.)

Seven

On Wings of Spruce

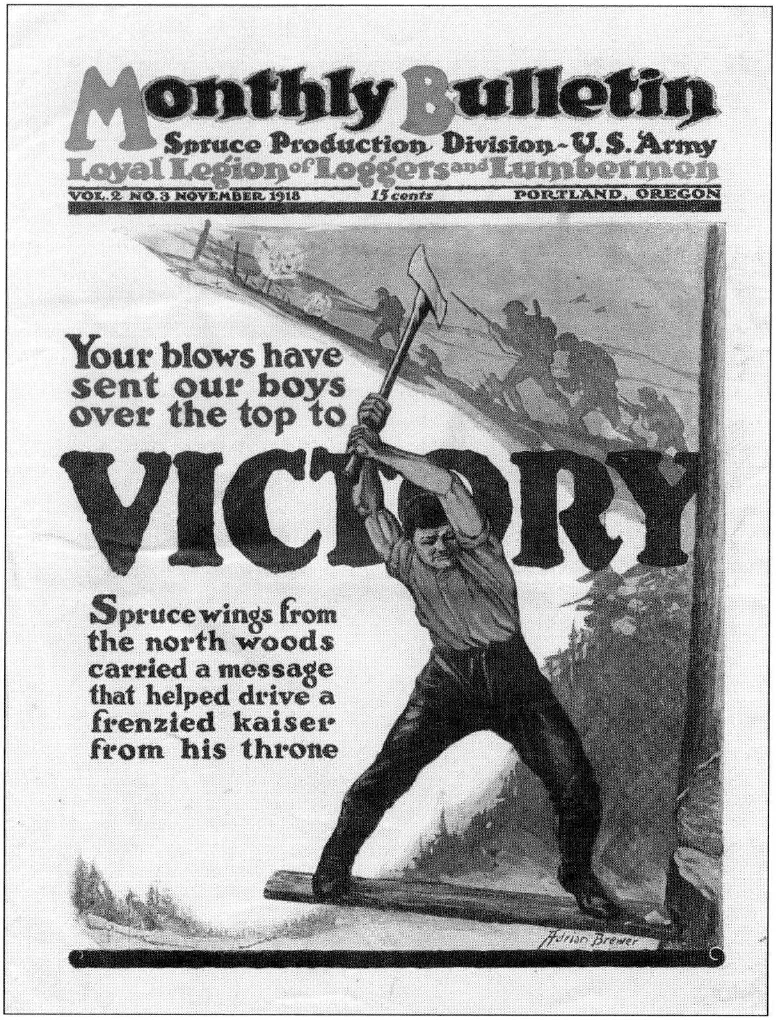

During World War I (1914–1918), manufacturers in Europe and America needed millions of feet of lumber from Sitka spruce for making airplanes. This chapter describes why they needed that wood and how loggers and mills on the Oregon coast helped meet the demand. Quotations on the following pages come from Brig. Gen. Brice Disque's *History of the Spruce Production Division*, published by the US Army in 1919. (Courtesy of OSU.)

As soon as World War I started in Europe, orders for spruce from factories in England, France, and America flooded mills in Oregon and Washington. The airframes of the de Havilland DH-4 (above) and the Curtiss Jenny (below) were made of wood, preferably spruce. The DH-4 was the first combat plane produced in America and was used for bombing and observation. Most planes built in America, almost 4,000, were made in Dayton, Ohio. The Curtiss Jenny, made in Buffalo, New York, was used primarily to train pilots. After the war, surplus Jennys became popular with stunt pilots. During the 1920s, many DH-4s were used for tests and training and to spot forest fires. In 1921, the US Postal Service started using DH-4s to launch airmail service. (Above, courtesy of OSU; below, courtesy of the author.)

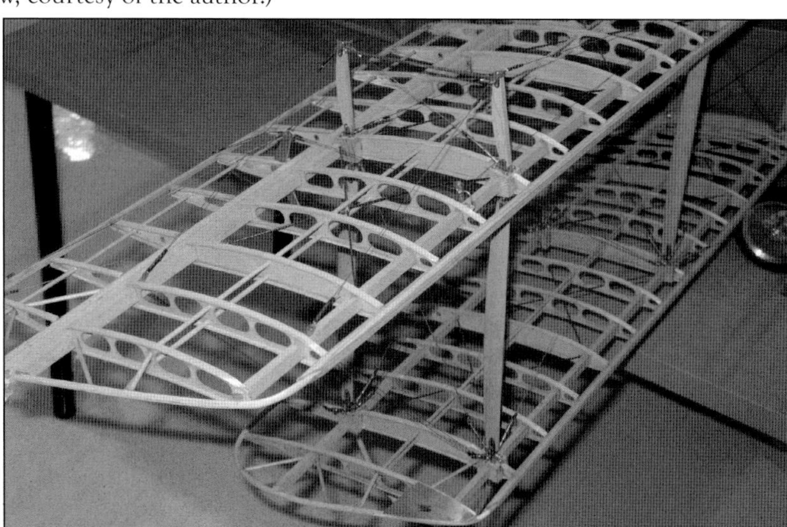

When America entered the war, the US Army sent officers and soldiers to the Northwest to take over spruce production. Soldiers supplemented civilian labor in the camps and mills essential to the war effort. In the image above, soldiers drill in front of the mill in Brighton on Nehalem Bay. When the war ended in November 1918, the Spruce Production Division (SPD) had 7,582 men in the forests and mills on the Oregon coast and 536 at headquarters in Portland. Washington had another 10,320 in forests and mills plus 9,388 operating the cut mill in Vancouver. Almost 28,000 soldiers bucked, rived, shipped, and milled spruce. The map below shows the numbers in the three Oregon districts, each with its own command structure. (Above, courtesy of Tillamook; below, courtesy of OSU.)

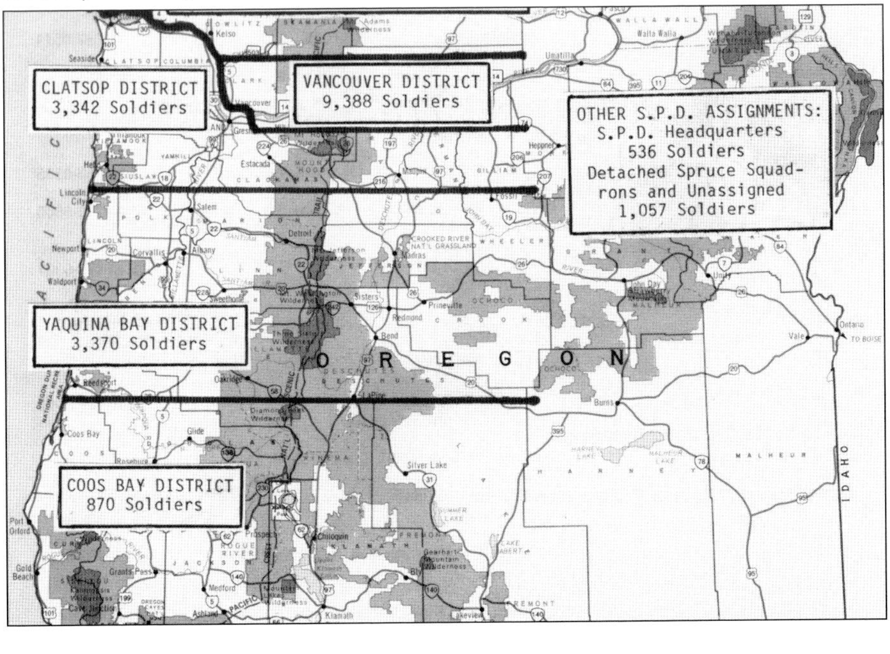

Army officers thought spruce was the perfect wood. Spruce is tough, light, and will not splinter from the impact of a bullet. It is strong but not brittle. Much of spruce has straight grain with no flaws. General Disque wrote, "We needed thousands and thousands of board feet of spruce. So an army was sent to make war in the virgin forest, a vast industrial machine built, and a great story of daring initiative and patient resourcefulness carved out. Spruce was the ally of the Allies. To take this giant from the air where he has towered for so many generations, to fall him to the ground, to lay him low: and then to impart lightness, speed, action, and restore him to the sky from whence he came—that was the task of the Spruce Production Division." (Courtesy of OSU.)

This spruce with loggers in the undercut might have scaled at 30,000 board feet—nice, but not huge by spruce standards. To make the undercut here, the loggers brought their saw and axes to the third level of springboards. Uniforms reveal the men were military, while the size of their chips and undercut reveal they were also experienced loggers. Logs in the image below, scaled at 28,000 board feet, could have come from that tree. General Disque wrote, "In the dark forests of Oregon, far removed from the sound and sight and stench of battle, men in khaki toiled valiantly over a task with nothing of the glamor of war—only the ring of the axe, the sing of the saw, the crash of falling timber. Those men were forging the weapon that would beat the hammers of the Teuton Thor." (Both, courtesy of OSU.)

General Disque assured readers that "Airplanes can be made of pine, hemlock or fir, but none compares to spruce. A Liberty engine will drive a two-seated deHavilland 147 miles per hour when made of spruce but slower when made of heavier materials. Spruce is essential. Thus to the army of builders fell the honor of writing one of the most splendid chapters of America's part in the war. The part was obscure and lacked thrill and romance. No man was cited for bravery to make good reading in school histories of the future. There was only dirty work and plenty of it. But men sent into the air must know they have the strongest wings nature, working with human ingenuity, can provide." (Left, courtesy of Tillamook; below, courtesy of OSU.)

Shortly after taking over spruce production, officers ordered riving in the woods instead of sending logs to mills. Riving required using axes, wedges, pry bars, and jacks to split logs along the grain. Riving jacks worked like the jacks used to lift cars to change tires, a task drivers faced often when early cars ran on thin tires on rough roads. Riving was expensive and wasteful but considered justifiable as a war measure. Splitting the log reduced the size of timber to about one-sixth of the original log. Such pieces could be hauled out of the woods by horses to an existing county road, put on trucks, and taken to the nearest railroad. (Above, courtesy of Tillamook; below, courtesy of Clatsop.)

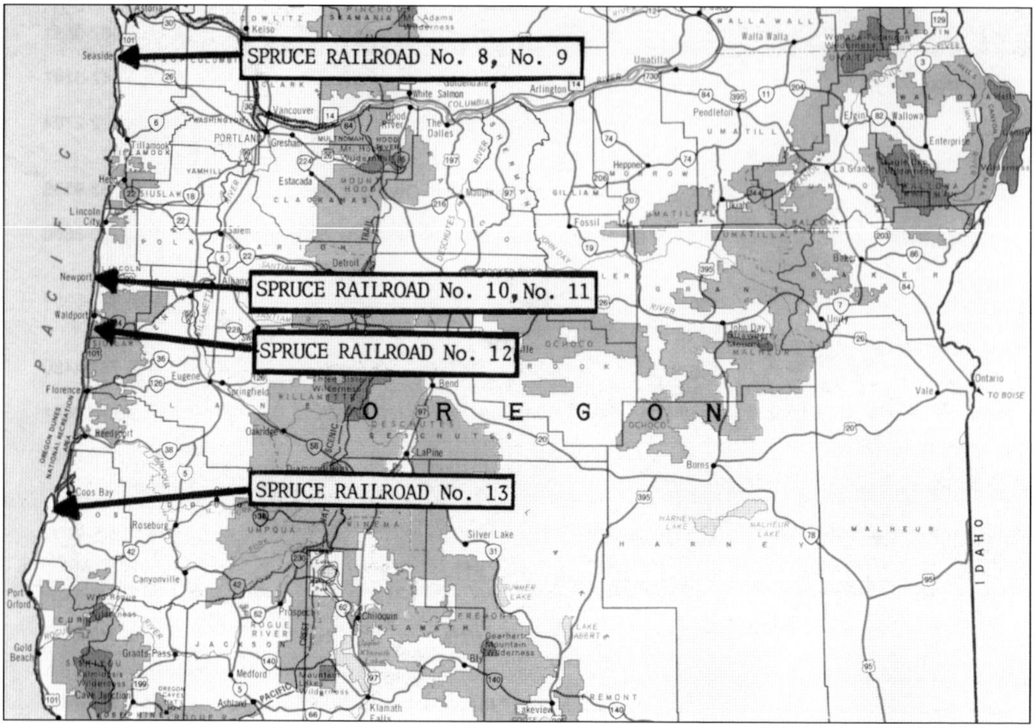

In the summer of 1918, the Spruce Production Division built five railroads into the coastal forests. Crews built the roads under the most difficult conditions. Lack of enough building equipment, steep cuts, and saturated soils made the work doubly hard in the rough country. Men placed 60- and 80-pound rails by hand. General Disque wrote, "Completion in a short time credits engineers doing the planning and soldiers doing the sweating." (Courtesy of OSU.)

General Disque described what his staff learned that local loggers knew by experience. "The country is magnificent. The grandeur of the forests lies but a step from the surf. But for logging operations, the same country leaves much to be desired. Water courses of all sizes seam the sides of the great hills which rise, often abruptly, from the shore to heights of a thousand, two thousand, even five thousand feet." (Courtesy of Tillamook.)

Soldiers grading for railroads sometimes began work before getting legal rights-of-way. Much of the land had been bought for speculation, platted in tiny parcels as summer resorts, and sold to people in the east who had never seen tidelands. Taxes had lapsed, sometimes for 20 years. If the military could not find owners, officers worked with county officials to buy the land through foreclosure. (Courtesy of Clatsop.)

Soldiers load ties to send to the railhead. Sixty miles of permanent railroads the military built in 1918 required over 200,000 ties. Spur lines needed thousands more. Mills all along the coast used the Douglas fir abundant in the forests to make ties, lumber to build camps, and other products vital to the war effort. (Courtesy of Clatsop.)

Workers used the handcarts in the foreground, also called "pumpers," to ferry tools and employees to sites along the tracks. Two men pumping hard could make a loaded cart go almost 10 miles an hour on level grades. Handcarts became obsolete in the 1920s, as gasoline-powered speeders and crummies took over their jobs. (Courtesy of Clatsop.)

Every day, workers built two miles of track for Railroad No. 12 south of Waldport. The railroads cost $30,000 per mile for labor and material, including 15 million board feet for trestles, ties, and camps. Building the railroads involved 4,200 soldiers and civilians working out of 33 construction camps. The SPD was exempt from rationing supplies for logging, such as rope and oil, and for loggers, such as shoes and waterproof cloth. (Courtesy of Clatsop.)

The large log in this image probably weighed six tons. But only the heartwood, about 10 percent, might prove acceptable for airplanes. Spruce trees have a twist in the outer part of the log, but grain for airplanes must not deflect more than one inch in 20. Mills could not cut wing beams 20, 22, and 24 feet long from trees growing with a spiral grain. (Courtesy of OSU.)

As railroads pushed into the woods, so did roads made for trucks using gasoline engines. Early gas engines could not match steam locomotives for pulling loads or climbing steep inclines, but building wooden roads for trucks cost much less than building railroads needing steel. And individual trucks meant more flexibility than lines of railcars. The activity shown in this image comes nowhere close to modern safety standards. (Courtesy of National Archives.)

Army data showed there was only one good airplane spruce to every five acres. Data showed the average spruce log is four feet in diameter and must measure 22 feet long for aircraft lumber. Needing 10 million feet of aircraft lumber a month meant moving 70 million feet of logs, or 192,000 tons, for an average distance of 20 miles through mountains, with most not even having wagon roads. (Courtesy of Tillamook.)

Whether in the form of cants or logs, the SPD sent all airplane spruce to a mill in Vancouver, Washington, which Army contractors built to cut wood to aircraft specifications. Local mills lacked machines and expertise for the job. This image shows a truckload of rived cants in Tillamook, where the mainline railroad would start its journey to the mill in Vancouver. (Courtesy of Tillamook.)

The mountains east of Newport yielded so much prime spruce that the mills in Toledo and Siletz could hardly keep up, especially with constantly changing specifications according to airplane design. Officers solved the problem by ordering the mills to cut cants, pieces ready for the specialized mill in Vancouver. The image above shows a paddle-wheel tug towing a raft of logs along the Yaquina River at Toledo ready for milling. Tents of the SPD camp appear at the far left of the image and in detail on page 125. The image below shows cants delivered by rail to the Port of Yaquina loading dock ready to send into the ocean and back up the Columbia River to Vancouver. More about the Vancouver mill can be found on page 126. (Above, courtesy of Tillamook; below, courtesy of OSU.)

In the spring of 1918, the Army needed 10 million board feet of spruce per month. The Vancouver mill could not meet that demand, so officers started two more mills closer to the timber, with one in Port Angeles, Washington, and one in Toledo, Oregon. Toledo could produce one million board feet per day and was 70 percent finished by the fall of 1918, but it closed when the war ended. After the war, the Pacific Spruce Corporation purchased the government's timber holdings in Lincoln County, the Toledo mill, the government railroads, and all the operations equipment. The new owner expanded the mill and coordinated its three corporate divisions—logging, lumber, and railroad—during the 1920s to ship millions of board feet from Toledo. (Courtesy of Siuslaw National Forest.)

Plans for the mill at Toledo called for a primary mill cutting cants and a second plant making airplane stock. Three railroads were to deliver 900,000 feet of logs each day. Production capacity would be 300,000 board feet per day when the mill opened and 800,000 per day by January 1919. Almost a thousand soldiers building and working at the mill lived in the tents in this image. (Courtesy of OSU.)

Military exemption from rationing extended to food. Quartermasters quickly convinced local suppliers that military needs took priority over civilian appetites. Generous budgets helped make the case. Quality and quantity of food, always expected by loggers, created incentives for civilian workers to apply for work and stay on the job. Working for the military also meant exemption from the draft. (Courtesy of OSU.)

In just 45 days, contractors built the huge mill in Vancouver. Covering 50 acres, the mill employed 3,000 soldiers working 24 hours per day, six days per week. By the fall of 1918, the mill could produce one million board feet a day and had not yet reached full capacity. But when the war ended in November, officers ordered demolition. The model in the image above at Pearson Air Museum in Vancouver represents the size and complexity of the structure. General Disque's final report said, "At the end of the war the Division owned everything in lumber from a box of toothpicks to 13,000 acres of timber. Everything from a stove bolt to a locomotive, a can of tomatoes to a railroad, a wrench to a sawmill, and timber perpendicular in forests, horizontal in mill ponds, and lumber cut to commercial sizes. One hundred fifty million feet of logs were in various stages from tree to the mill. Large equipment included 400 donkey engines, 350 automobiles, trucks and trailers, five motor launches, 18 locomotives, five locomotive cranes, 14,000 tons of rails, and many tons of machines and supplies for sawmills. All sold at surplus prices to civilian markets." (Courtesy of the author.)

BIBLIOGRAPHY

Andrews, Ralph. *Timber: Toil and Trouble in the Big Woods*. Seattle: Superior Publishing, 1968.
Churchill, Sam. *Big Sam*. Garden City, NJ: Doubleday, 1965.
———. *Don't Call Me Ma*. Garden City, NJ: Doubleday, 1977.
Conway, F.D., and Gail Wells. *Timber in Oregon: History and Projected Trends*. Corvallis: Oregon State University Press, 1993.
Cox, Thomas. *Mills and Markets: A History of the Pacific Coast Lumber Industry to 1900*. Seattle: University of Washington Press, 1974.
Disque, Brice P. *History of the Spruce Production Division, United States Army and United States Spruce Production Corporation*. Portland: Kilham Printing for US Army, 1919.
Gibbons, William. *Logging in the Douglas Fir Region*. Washington, DC: US Department of Agriculture bulletin 711, 1918.
Holbrook, Stewart. *Holy Old Mackinaw: Natural History of an American Logger*. New York: Macmillan, 1938.
Jensen, Vernon. *Lumber and Labor*. New York: Farrar and Rinehart, 1945.
Kamholz, Edward. *The Oregon-American Lumber Company Ain't No More*. Palo Alto, CA: Stanford University Press, 2003.
LeMonds, James. *Deadfall: Generations of Loggers in the Pacific Northwest*. Missoula, MT: Mountain Press, 2001.
Lucia, Ellis. *The Big Woods: Logging and Lumbering from Bull Teams to Helicopters in the Pacific Northwest*. New York: Knopf, 1975.
McCulloch, Walter. *Woods Words: A Comprehensive Dictionary of Loggers' Terms*. Portland: Oregon Historical Society, 1958.
Newell, Gordon. *Pacific Lumber Ships*. Seattle: Superior Publishing, 1960.
Prouty, Andrew. *More Deadly than War! Pacific Coast Logging, 1827–1981*. New York: Garland Publishing, 1985.
Robbins, William. *Hard Times in Paradise: Coos Bay, Oregon, 1850–1986*. Seattle: University of Washington Press, 1980.
Strite, Daniel. "Up the Kilchis." *Oregon Historical Quarterly* 72, no. 4 (December 1971): 292-314; 73, no. 1 (March 1972): 5-30; 73, no. 2 (June 1972): 171–192; 73, no. 3 (September 1972): 212–227.
Van Tassel, Alfred J. *Mechanization in the Lumber Industry*. Washington, DC: WPA National Research Report M-5, 1940.